THE GREAT AMERICAN BOOK OF

Church Signs

Photography by Donald Seitz

Publishing Company
Sock And Roll Corporation
900 20th Avenue South, Suite 614
Nashville, TN 37212

978-0-9789715-1-9

DEDICATION

To Mom and Dad who started the adventure.

To my wife, Maureen, and my son, William, who make the journey so sweet.

And to God who holds the maps.

GREATER PLEASANT VIEW
BAPTIST CHURCH

HE WHO KNEELS
BEFORE GOD CAN STAND
BEFORE ANYONE.

SUNDAY SCHOOL 10:00AM
WORSHIP SERVICE 11:15AM

Celebrating **100 YEARS**
1894 - 1994

Brentwood, Tennessee

FOREWORD

Church signs are part of the American cultural landscape. Like brilliant wildflowers or persistent weeds, church signs edge the borders of our highways, streets, and backroads. You'll see them almost anywhere — rising from Kentucky corn fields, shadowed by California palms, standing firm in Louisiana bogs, or even clinging to a stone wall on New York's Fifth Avenue. Americans may not wear their faith on their sleeves, but they love to show it on the road.

By "church signs" I don't mean the plain marquees that display Sunday's sermon schedule. Instead, I'm talking about those bold, often unruly looking signboards that have slots for large, black, moveable type. The perfect template for dishing out a pithy sermon, like, "Know God, no sin," or "Exercise daily, walk with the Lord." There's nothing static about these signs. They're meant to change, and they usually change weekly. Sometimes daily, if a gust of wind shakes loose a dangling "k," and what was once an intended "know" becomes an accidental or perhaps divinely inspired "now."

Church signs are meant to challenge as well as change. They confront their readers to live better lives, to love more deeply, to pray more often. And they're aimed at the kind of audience that every advertising executive dreams about — a captive one. It's hard to avert your eyes to these signs of faith. It's not like the car radio where you can flip the dial if you don't like what's on. Church signs act like powerful spiritual magnets, drawing you in for a closer look, for a sacred moment of reflection.

Or sometimes for just a laugh. Church signs are often one-liners, with the rhythm, timing, and delivery of a vaudeville performer. Puns are popular. "This church is prayer conditioned" comes to mind. Poking fun at the human condition is fair game too, as in, "A sharp tongue and a dull mind are usually found in the same head." And of course, like the bad stand-up comic who needs the hook, some signs are downright groaners, blessedly removed from public sight by the Monday morning commute.

Every sign tells its own story, revealing a rich variety of wisdom, wit and faith. In some photos, the words say it all. In others, the message is in the details — like the beer truck in the background, the ominous desert sky, or the father and son in the doorway. Collectively, these church signs offer one great American sermon.

I hope you will enjoy this photographic journey of faith.

Donald Seitz

CONTENTS

BLAKEMORE
Church of the Nazarene

VISITORS   WELCOME
MEMBERS   EXPECTED

Nashville, Tennessee

Faith & Forgiveness

Now faith is the assurance of things hoped for, and the conviction of things not seen. (Hebrews 11:1)

It seems hard to sneak a look at God's hand.
Albert Einstein

Killen, Alabama

CHURCH OF CHRIST
at BROOKHILL

SUNDAY BIBLE STUDY 9 AM   WORSHIP 10 AM
SUNDAY EVENING 6 PM   WED. EVENING 7 PM
SORROW LOOKS BACK
WORRY LOOKS AROUND
AND
FAITH LOOKS UP

Killen, Alabama

Council Bluffs, Iowa

Lynchburg, Virginia

West Brattleboro, Vermont

Blythewood, South Carolina

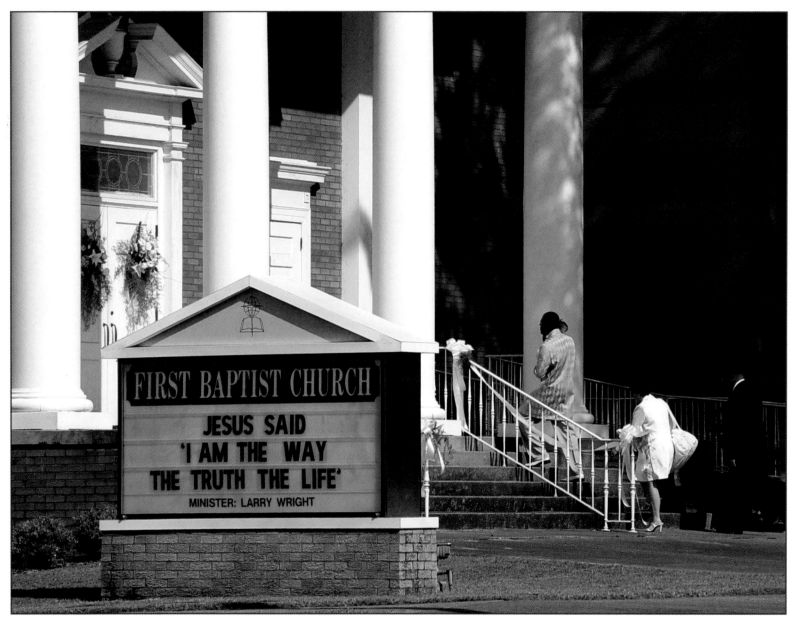

Florence, Alabama

ST. JOSEPH PARISH SERVICE CENTER

PSALMS READ HERE

St. Joseph's is a stewardship parish!

Hays, Kansas

Russellville, Kentucky

Athens, Georgia

Westmoreland, Tennessee

Fayettville, Tennessee

† Wilhoit Southern Baptist Church

THE BEST WAY TO
GET EVEN IS TO
FORGIVE AND FORGET

SUN 945 1055 600
WED 600

Kirkland, Arizona

East Bernstadt, Kentucky

Atkins, Virginia

Montpelier, Vermont

Chattanooga, Tennessee

SOUTH CHURCH
UNITARIAN UNIVERSALIST

WORSHIP
SERVICE

RELIGIOUS
EDUCATION

True religion is the
life we lead, not the
creed we profess.

—Louis Nizer

Portsmouth, New Hampshire

Frankfort, Michigan

GOD MAY MEET
YOU TODAY
WHERE YOU
LEAST EXPECT
HIM

Salina, Kansas

First Baptist Church

WE NEED TO TALK....

GOD

Camden, Arkansas

The sign reads:

Tompkinsville
Church of Christ

SUNDAY 9-10AM 6PM
WEDNESDAY 7PM
WHEN IT COMES TO GIVING
SOME PEOPLE
STOP AT NOTHING

Advice & Admonitions

Draw near to God and He will draw near to you. (James 4:8)

Do all the good you can, and make as little fuss as possible.
Charles Dickens

Collinwood, Tennessee

Lindon, Utah

Nashville, Tennessee

Starkville, Mississippi

Lewisburg, Tennessee

Lubbock, Texas

NO MAN IS RICH ENOUGH
TO BUY BACK HIS PAST

Junction City, Louisiana

YOUNG MEMORIAL
UNITED METHODIST CHURCH

WORRY IS INTEREST PAID
ON TROUBLE
BEFORE IT IS DUE

Thomson, Georgia

Manchester, New Hampshire

Brentwood, Tennessee

Vienna, Illinois

TRINITY LUTHERAN CHURCH ELCA
SUNDAYS 8:30 & 11AM
JOIN US
TO BELITTLE
IS TO BE LITTLE

KIDS WELCOME HERE

Evanston, Illinois

Nashville, Tennessee

WEST END
CHURCH of CHRIST

WORRY IS THE DARKROOM
IN WHICH NEGATIVES
ARE DEVELOPED

Sunday   Bible Class 9:00am   Wednesday Bible Class 6:30pm
         Worship 10:00am

Nashville, Tennessee

Portsmouth, New Hampshire

Auburn, Kentucky

VICTORY BAPTIST CHURCH

CHARACTER IS HOW YOU TREAT THOSE WHO CAN DO NOTHING FOR YOU.

WORSHIP SERVICE WED. PRAYER & BIBLE
BIBLE CLASSES   11:00 AM & 6:00 PM   :00 P   - 877-3393
9:45 AM

Vergennes, Vermont

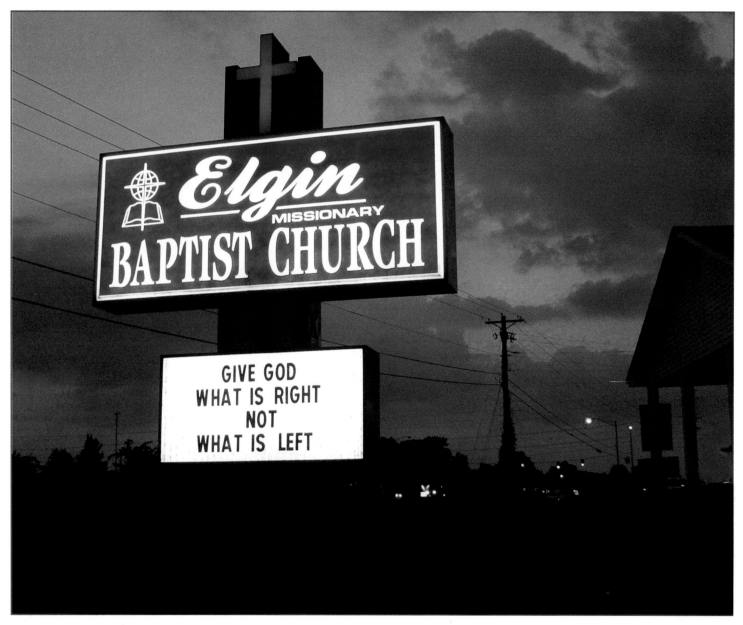

Rogersville, Alabama

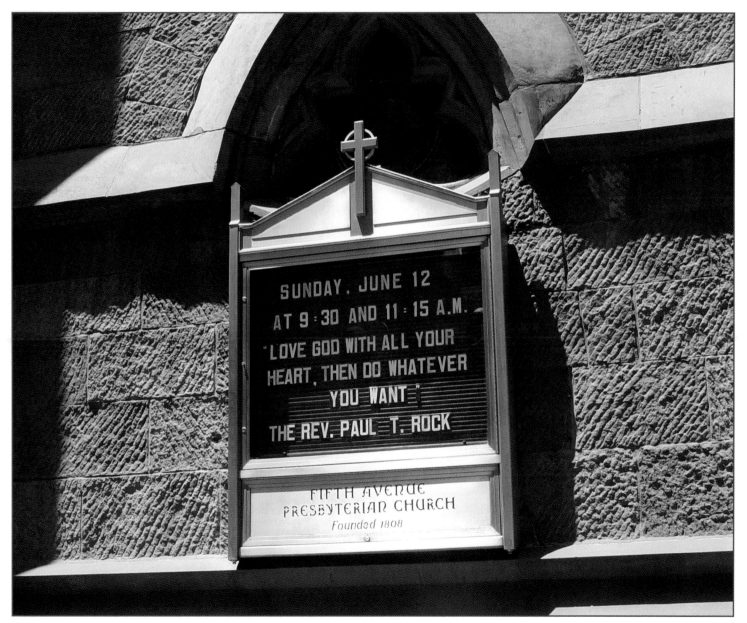

New York, New York

Prayer & Perserverance

Be anxious for nothing, but in all things by prayer and supplication with thanksgiving,

let your requests be known unto God. (Philippians 4:6)

Pray to God but continue to row to the shore.
Russian Proverb

Auburn, Georgia

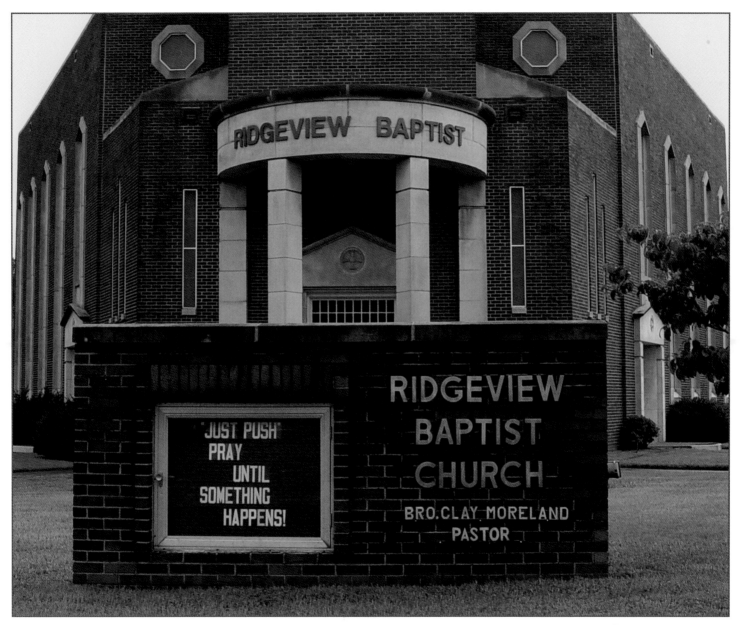

Chattanooga, Tennessee

Nashville, Tennessee

CHRIST UNITED METHODIST CHURCH
AND PRESCHOOL

SUNDAY SCHOOL
9:30AM

WORSHIP
8:00, 9:30, & 10:45AM

FAILING IS NOT FALLING DOWN
IT IS STAYING DOWN

301

O'DEA
SCHOOL

Ft. Collins, Colorado

Brentwood, Tennessee

Santa Monica, California

Berkeley Heights, New Jersey

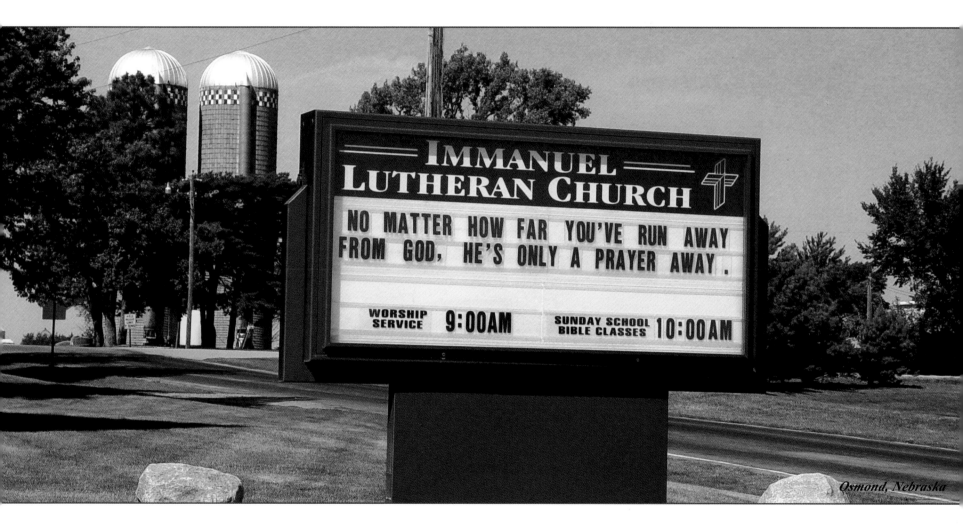

IMMANUEL
LUTHERAN CHURCH

NO MATTER HOW FAR YOU'VE RUN AWAY
FROM GOD, HE'S ONLY A PRAYER AWAY.

WORSHIP
SERVICE 9:00AM

SUNDAY SCHOOL
BIBLE CLASSES 10:00AM

Osmond, Nebraska

63

Eagle Mills, Arkansas

Salina, Kansas

McConnells, South Carolina

WEST END CHURCH of CHRIST

DON'T GIVE UP. MOSES WAS ONCE A BASKET CASE.

Sunday
Bible Class 9:00am
Worship 10:00am

Wednesday Bible Class 6:3

Gentle-Ride Van

Nashville, Tennessee

Light & Love

He who does not love does not know God, for God is love. (1 John 4:8)

Be glad of life because it gives you a chance to love
and to work and to play and to look up at the stars.
Henry Van Dyke

Clinton, Mississippi

CHURCH OF CHRIST
AT ELKTON

| BIBLE STUDY | SUNDAY WORSHIP | WEDNESDAY |
| 10:00 AM | 11:00 AM & 6:00 PM | 7:00 PM |

LIVE WELL
LAUGH OFTEN
LOVE MUCH

Elkton, Tennessee

Tompkinsville, Kentucky

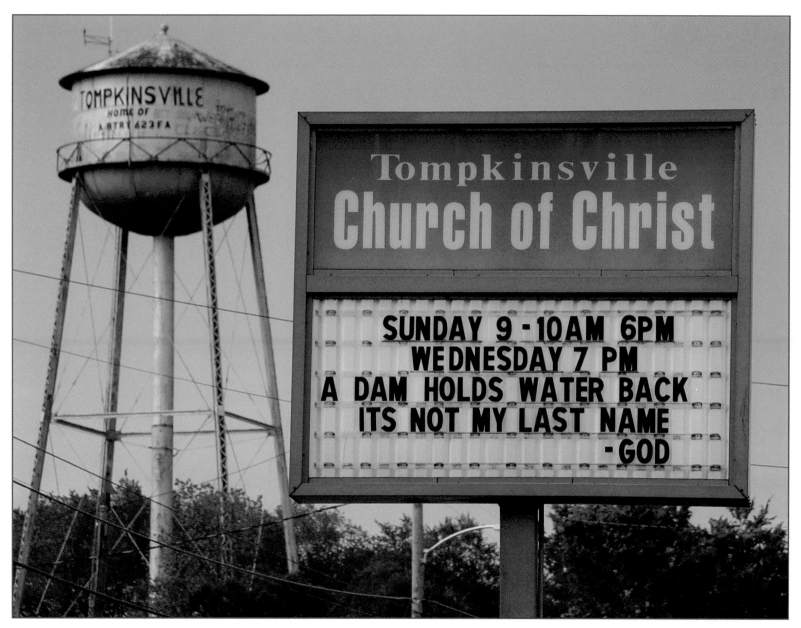

Tompkinsville, Kentucky

Springfield, Kentucky

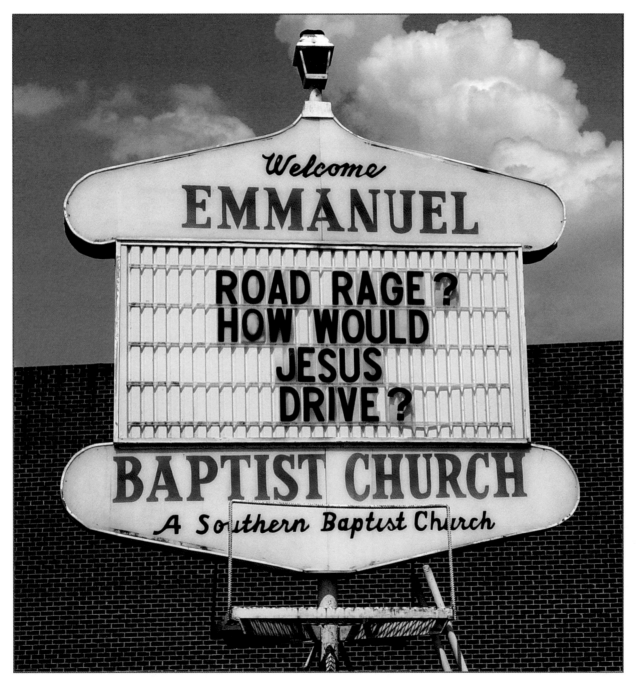

Monroe, Louisiana

Indianapolis, Indiana

Cleveland, Ohio

Florence, Alabama

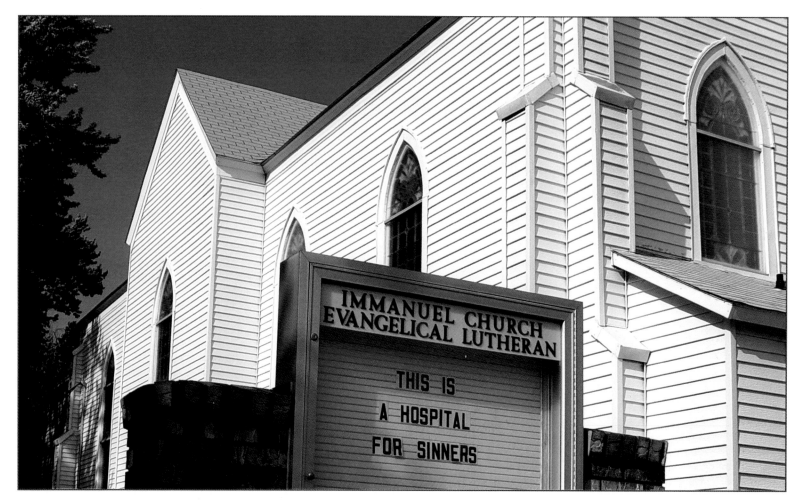

Hadar, Nebraska

Frankfort, Michigan

St. Louis, Missouri

SUN   1130AM

SERMON

THIS TOO WILL PASS

Billings, Montana

Monroe, Louisiana

Omaha, Nebraska

First Baptist Church

Rev. James Peach • Sun. Sch. 9:45 am • Service 11:00am 6:00pm • Wed. 6:00 pm

A GRATEFUL MIND
IS A
GREAT MIND

Vega, Texas

Nashville, Tennessee

Tompkinsville, Kentucky

Staunton, Virginia

Florence, Alabama

NEW PROSPECT
BAPTIST CHURCH

EVERYONE NEEDS TO BE LOVED
ESPECIALLY WHEN THEY DONT
DESERVE   IT

Dubach, Louisiana

Wytheville, Virginia

Eternity

The grass withers and the flower falls, but the Word of the Lord endures forever. (1 Peter 1:24, 25)

Eternity. It's not the end of the world.
It's the world without end.
Author Unknown

Brent, Alabama

Nashville, Tennessee

St. Louis, Missouri

Sylvan Park, Tennessee

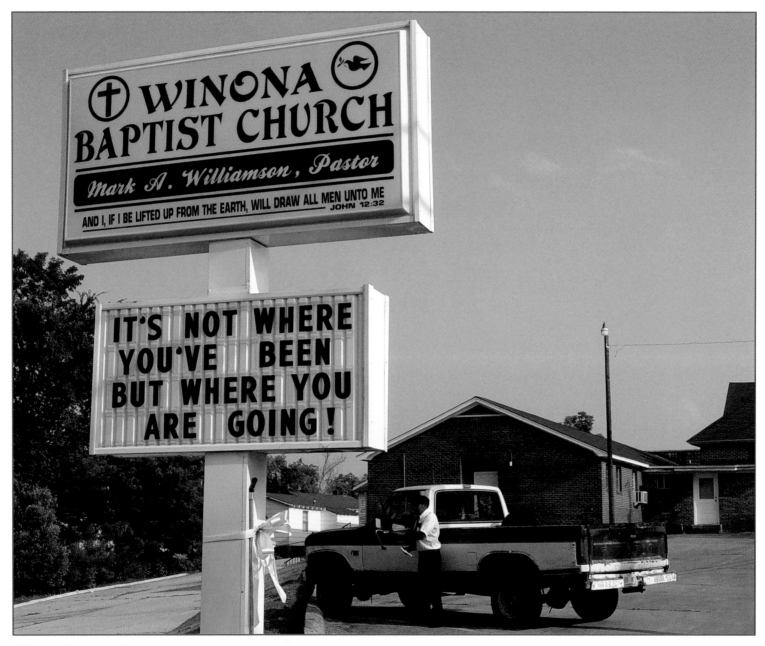

Winona, Mississippi

100

Lafayette, Indiana

EAST UNION
CHRISTIAN CHURCH

DONT LET OUR PAST
DICTATE WHO YOU ARE
LET IT BE PART OF
WHO YOU WILL BECOME

Atlanta, Indiana

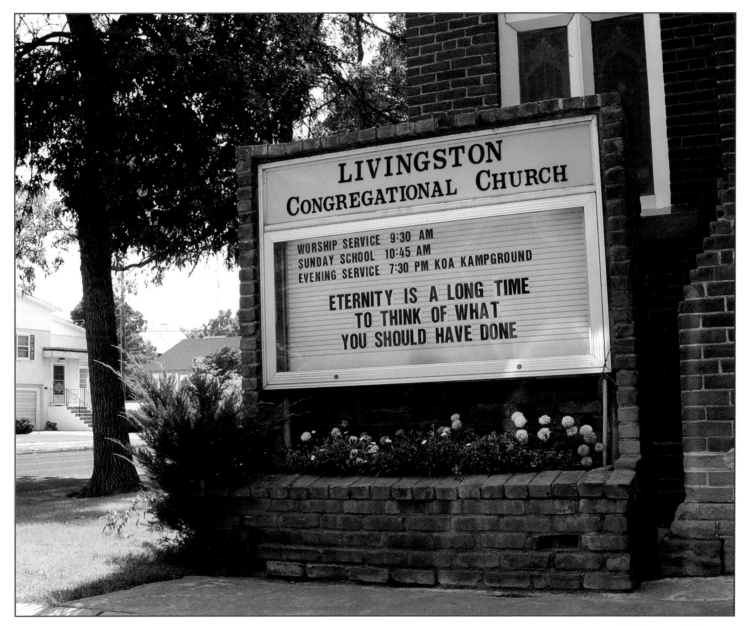

LIVINGSTON
CONGREGATIONAL CHURCH

WORSHIP SERVICE 9:30 AM
SUNDAY SCHOOL 10:45 AM
EVENING SERVICE 7:30 PM KOA KAMPGROUND

ETERNITY IS A LONG TIME
TO THINK OF WHAT
YOU SHOULD HAVE DONE

Livingston, Montana

Galax, Virginia

Paint Lick, Kentucky

West Monroe, Louisiana

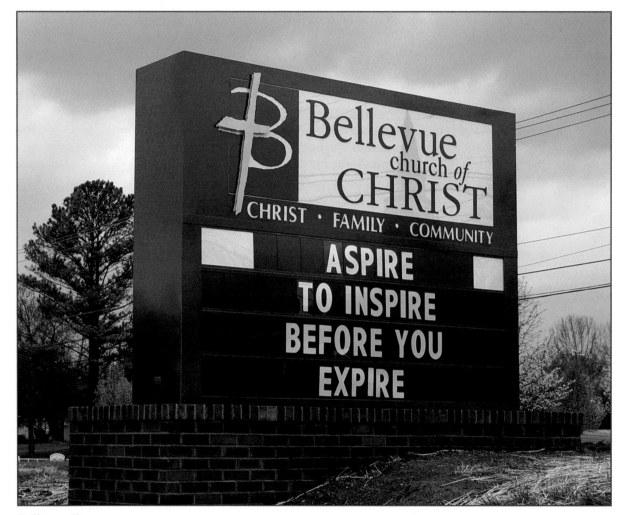

Bellevue, Tennessee

Stromsburg, Nebraska

POSTSCRIPT

If brevity is the soul of wit, it is also the heart of faith—at least on the road.
The average church sign is eight words long.

Many thanks to all of the churches whose signs appear here, and to the thousands of churches
across America that display daily words of faith, encouragement, and humor. Special thanks to the
Greater Pleasant View Baptist Church in Brentwood, Tennessee, whose sign inspired the making of this book,
and to the United Pentecostal Church of East Nashville, Tennessee, whose sign inspired the cover art.

Have your travels taken you by a favorite church sign?
I'd love to hear how you have been moved by just a few words of faith.

Email: donaldseitz@bellsouth.net
www.thisisyoursign.com

Twelve More From The Road

Can't sleep? Try counting your blessings.

To get a better preacher, pray for the one you got.

You can't grow an oak tree in a flower pot.

All sunshine makes a desert.

Don't worry about tomorrow--you did that yesterday.

A living is what you get. A life is what you give.

Heaven. Don't miss it for the world.

An apology is a good way to have the last word.

We don't have a prayer without God.

Triumph is "umph" added to try.

Leaning on God is like learning to float.

You can't give away kindness. It always comes back.

Red Boiling Springs, Tennessee